Superstars! Superstars! Superstars! Superstars!

CREATIVE EDUCATION SPORTS SUPERSTARS

te rosepete ros
osepete ro
ete rosepet
rosepete ro

rosepete ros
rosepete pet
pete rosepet
pete rosepet
pete pete ro
rosepete ro

pete rose

by James P. Smith

CREATIVE EDUCATION
CHILDRENS PRESS

PHOTO CREDITS

Bruce Curtis: Cover, 7, 10, 13, 28
Carl Skalak, Jr.: 8, 16, 21, 24

Published by Creative Educational Society, Inc., 123 South Broad Street, Mankato, Minnesota 56001. Copyright © 1977 by Creative Educational Society, Inc. International copyrights reserved in all countries. No part of this book may be reproduced in any form without written permission from the publisher. Printed in the United States.

Library of Congress Cataloging in Publication Data

Smith, James Philip, 1935-
Pete Rose.

—Juvenile literature.

1. Rose, Pete, 1942-   —Juvenile literature.
2. Baseball players—United States—Biography—Juvenile literature. I. Title.
GV865.R65S63   796.357′092′4 [B]   76-46396
ISBN 0-87191-540-5

U.S. 1959288

The 1975 World Series was one of the most exciting Series ever. Even before the last game started, there had been enough close calls, brilliant plays and dramatic situations to talk about for years. But for the Cincinnati Reds, waiting for the seventh game was very frustrating.

The Reds knew, down deep, that they were the best team in baseball. They also knew that they still had to

prove this to a lot of doubters, because they had been in the World Series in 1970 and 1972, and had lost both times. In 1975, they were supposed to have beaten the Red Sox in six games. But here they were, going into a seventh game. This could be their last chance.

No one felt this pressure more keenly than Pete Rose, the Cincinnati third baseman, and no one was more determined than he to make sure that this time they would not be denied the prize. He played fiercely in the first six games, and was really ready for the seventh.

He began to go to work in the sixth inning, with one out. The Reds had fallen behind, 3-0. Their dream was becoming dim, and even their confidence was beginning to sag. When Rose came to bat, it was clearly up to him to do something.

The Boston fans knew how often Pete had ignited rallies in late innings, and they grew restless. Then Pete did just what they feared he would do. He singled, smashing a hard shot through the infield.

Not only did this put Pete on first, it brought Johnny Bench to the plate. Bench is one of the best catchers in baseball and is always a threat to hit a long ball. Bench connected, the crowd roared. It was a weak

ground ball to the Red Sox shortstop. The Red Sox fans anticipated a double play that would not only put out the rally and end the inning, but perhaps it would finally break the Reds' spirit. Then the crowd gasped.

Just as the Red Sox shortstop flipped the ball to second baseman Denny Doyle, Pete came barreling into the bag. His slide forced Doyle into an awkward throwing position, and Doyle's throw to first base went all the way into the first base dugout instead. Rose was out, but Bench moved to second.

When the throw went into the dugout, a shudder could be felt all over Fenway Park in Boston. Something went out of the Red Sox. Everyone knew that, despite the score, it was a brand new game.

The Reds breathed easier, sensing somehow that they were now on their way; it took them only a minute to capitalize on the new situation.

The missed double play seemed to affect Red Sox pitcher Bill Lee. On his second pitch to Tony Perez, the Reds' first baseman, Lee threw what he said was his only bad pitch of the game. He threw the ball hard toward home plate, but Perez hit it back even harder. He hit it over the net in left-center field for a two-run home run. That made it 3-2, and the Reds were back in the game for real.

Pete Rose was not through yet. In the eighth, with the score still 3-2, Ken Griffey singled, stole second, and waited for Pete to do something again. Pete waited for the pitch, crouching over the plate. Then he uncoiled and drilled a line drive to center field, scoring Griffey with the tying run. The Reds' momentum was obvious to everyone now; once again they were the Big Red Machine.

The Red Sox did show a brief sign of life in their half of the eighth. Dwight Evans walked, and the Red Sox fans sat up in their seats, waiting and hoping. But again Rose took over. The next batter hit a ground ball to his left, and Pete started a quick double play, third to second to first. To round out the inning, he made the third out when he easily handled a high pop foul. The eighth inning belonged to Pete.

There was no longer any question whether the Reds would win it. The only question now was how they would do it. The answer came quickly. In the ninth, Griffey walked, went to second on a sacrifice, and moved to third on an infield out. This time the Red Sox pitcher was more careful with Pete, and he drew a base on balls.

Rose was frustrated at not getting the good ball to hit, but he wasn't disgruntled for long. He knew by now that even if he didn't get it, one of his teammates

would. As he sprinted to first, his friend, Joe Morgan, came up.

Sure enough, Morgan reached out, and with an easy, gentle swing, tapped the ball into shallow center field. Centerfielder Fred Lynn could not get to it in time to make the catch, nor could he make the throw to the plate quickly enough to nail the runner.

Griffey scored, putting the Reds ahead 4-3. They continued to threaten, ending the inning with the bases loaded. But they only needed that one run. The Red Sox went down in order in their half of the ninth, and the Reds were World Champions for the first time since 1941.

Pete's smashing play during the Series and his leadership earned for him the award as the World Series' Most Valuable Player. He hit safely ten times for an average of .370, scored three times, and played without error at third base. Time after time, he seemed to be in just the place where he was most needed.

Pete's teammates knew how much he had meant to their victory, and were glad when he received the award. But Pete knew how much it had been a team effort. When he received a sports car as part of the MVP prize, he said that he wished he could carve it into 26 pieces, one share for every player on the team.

There was a time, though, when Pete did not stand in such good terms with his Reds teammates. He was given a shot at making the team in the 1963 spring training, after spending three years in the minor leagues. Pete played every day as if his life depended on it. His aggressive, hustling play did not endear him to other members of the team, especially some of the veterans.

One day, the older players were wondering which of the rookies would make the final roster. They took a vote, and all but one felt that Pete would not make it. The only one who did think he would make it was Don Blasingame, the second baseman. Sadly for him, he was right: Pete soon took over Blasingame's position at second. Pete went on to hit .278, and was chosen the National League Rookie of the Year.

Gradually, people began to see that Pete was a hard-driving, intense and colorful player. They also saw that he had natural abilities to spare, and the confidence to play every phase of the game with the best of them. He had the makings of a complete baseball player.

For example, he has a rare talent that only the good hitters have. He can spot the kind of pitch from the

way the seams turn, and adjust his swing accordingly. When he is batting, of course, he doesn't take time to say to himself, "Well, the seams are rotating down and to the right from this lefty, so here comes a curve." Rather, he concentrates so hard that his response with the bat is immediate.

This takes super coordination. His hands, arms, legs and eyes all work together as a unit. When he swings, Pete's body is like a sprung trap. His eyes stay on the ball all the way. There is no wasted motion: the bat snaps into the ball.

He gets all kinds of hits: bunts, scratch bouncers, and bloopers, but mostly line drives. They go through the infield, over it, off the wall and sometimes over the wall.

If a count were kept, it would probably turn out that most of his hits go to center field. Stroking hits to center means that the batter is timing the pitch just right, keeping his eye on it, and meeting it squarely, just in front of the plate. A hit to center is a sign that in this particular hand-to-hand combat, the batter has outduelled the pitcher.

Pete uses his time at the plate efficiently. He does not have the habit of waiting for "just the right pitch." Instead, he "owns" the whole strike zone, and whatever comes through it. For Pete, if it is a strike, it is a good pitch to hit. The pitcher knows that when Pete crouches over the plate, he is being challenged: "Just try to get one over that I can't hit."

He is always ready to "find his strike," as he says, ready to hit the good pitches with the good part of the bat. The importance of this can be seen in what happened in the last stages of the 1969 season.

With two weeks to go, Pete had the second highest batting average in the National League. Eight percentage points ahead of him was Cleon Jones of the New York Mets. Cleon was injured, however, and had to sit out a few games.

Pete knew he could catch up with Cleon. He felt a splurge of base hits coming on, and believed that when Cleon started playing again, the Mets' outfielder would probably have some trouble finding his strike. Sure enough, Cleon got only two hits in his first 14 at bats, and his average dipped to .340.

Meanwhile, Pete was finding his strikes. He hit safely 18 times in 39 at bats and raised his average to .347. He finished the season as the league's number one hitter at .348, and was National League batting champion for the second straight year.

Rose is, in fact, one of the most productive hitters in

baseball history. By the end of the 1976 season, he will have almost 2750 hits. By the time he finishes playing as a Major Leaguer, he could even be getting close to Ty Cobb's record of 4191.

He will be the first switch-hitter to hit safely 3000 times. He already holds the record for most hits in a season by a switch-hitter, 230, which he set in 1973. Those 230 hits also included a record-setting 181 singles, and helped win for him the National League award as Most Valuable Player.

In 1974 and 1975, he led the league in runs scored with 110 and 112. At the end of his 12th season in 1975, he had scored 1329 runs. If he keeps up that pace, he will challenge another of Ty Cobb's seemingly untouchable records, Cobb's total of 2244 runs scored. He will need a lot of help from his teammates to break this record, but as long as he keeps getting on base and the Reds continue hitting, don't count him out.

Pete's play sets the pace for the Reds. He has infected them with a rough-and-tumble team spirit which keeps them "up." When they are playing well, they kid each other regularly and with gusto. As Joe Morgan put it, "We don't have the kind of guys who would let each other get complacent." When things are not going so well, they take a big breath and work together on making their plays start clicking again.

An incident seen on national television early in 1976 caught this spirit. Dave Concepcion, the Reds' gifted shortstop, bobbled a ball and the batter reached first safely. Concepcion was visibly upset with himself; he kicked the dirt and pounded his glove. Rose could be seen near third base, studying the next hitter, not saying anything to the shortstop.

In the next few minutes, Concepcion took over. He seemed to be all over the field. First he caught a pop fly near the left-field stands after a long run. Then he made an out-of-nowhere stop of a grounder deep to his right, and threw out the runner by a step.

As Concepcion and Rose jogged off the field, Pete held his glove to his face and said something to the shortstop. Concepcion glared back at Pete through narrowed eyes with mock fury on his face. Pete laughed. With the kind of ribbing that goes on among the Reds, Rose probably did *not* say, "Good play, Dave." More likely it was something like, "You'll do anything to make an easy play look tough, won't you?"

Sometimes Pete's spirited play gets him in trouble with both players and fans. He was involved in two famous incidents which for a while made him the "villain" of baseball.

The first happened in the 1970 All-Star game. In the twelfth inning, Pete was running full tilt from second with the winning run. He saw that Ray Fosse, the American League's catcher from Oakland, was blocking his way to the plate. They collided. Pete was irresistible, and Ray was movable. Pete scored, and the impact sent Ray tumbling to the ground. Both players were shaken. Pete went to Fosse to see if he was all right, as the catcher was holding his shoulder and shaking his head.

Pete's teammates swarmed all over him, congratulating him for scoring the winning run, and he didn't get a chance to talk to Ray. Fosse's left shoulder was badly bruised, and Pete suffered a swollen left knee.

The fans were hard on Pete for what they thought was an unnecessarily hard drive for the plate. The American League manager, Earl Weaver, disagreed. He said that both players had done what they had to do. And it was true; the two players had wanted the same thing, home plate.

The second incident occurred in 1973. In the third playoff game with the New York Mets, Pete slid into second base on the front end of a double play. Bud Harrelson, the Mets shortstop, took exception to the force of his slide. In a flash, the two were swinging at each other. Harrelson was the smaller of the two, but was joined by Mets' third baseman Wayne Garrett.

Both teams left their dugouts and converged on the dust cloud swelling up around second base. The fighting players were separated with difficulty. As Pete left the field, the crowd at Shea Stadium booed him mightily.

Pete did not seem to be bothered by the crowd's reaction. In fact he was buoyed up by all the controversy. He was going to show them just who Pete Rose was.

And the next day he did. He hit a home run to win the game in the 12th inning. Sagging into their seats, even the Mets fans were impressed. Pete whipped around the bases with his closed hand high above his head. There could be no doubt in anyone's mind: Pete Rose was the picture of pure competitive pride.

After the season, talk about the fight did not die down. Rose is not the kind of player who excites lukewarm emotions, and people's emotions were pretty well stirred up.

Rose and Harrelson were both invited to attend a sportswriters' banquet. Baseball fans wondered what would happen when they met. At the banquet Pete

walked up to Bud, took him by the shoulders, kissed him on the cheek and said he hoped there were no hard feelings. The audience exploded with delight. Pete loved it.

Harrelson, a tough pro himself, smiled and took it in stride. After all, he has known Pete for a long time and even admits to being a bit of a Rose fan. Harrelson not only admires Pete's ability, but remembers how Pete once helped him out. Pete suggested that the Mets' shortstop might do better with a smaller glove. Harrelson tried one, felt his play was improved, and has stayed with it.

There are, in fact, Pete Rose fans in every city in baseball. In Cincinnati they used to assemble in the stands behind his position in the outfield. The area became known as "The Rose Garden."

Fans have elected Pete to the National League All-Star team nine times. He has been an All-Star second baseman, left-fielder, right-fielder and, in 1976, a third baseman. His election in 1976 made him one of only three players ever to be chosen to play four different positions in All-Star games. He joins very select company; the other two are Henry Aaron and Stan Musial.

Pete performed in the 1976 All-Star game with his usual flair. He led off for the National League and bashed the first pitch up the middle for a single and eventually scored. Later he drove a liner to the wall in right center field, tore around the bases and dove into third on his stomach with a triple. Pete always gives his fans what they love to see.

This style of play is a legacy from Pete's father. Harry Rose, who was also known as "Pete," was an outstanding athlete throughout his life. He was active in organized sports and was recognized all over Cincinnati for his ability and leadership.

Harry Rose died unexpectedly in December, 1974. His death left Pete emotionally drained for a long time. Father and son had enjoyed an exceptionally close relationship. The whole baseball world was saddened.

In 1950, when Pete was nine years old, he began to play baseball in the Cincinnati Knothole League. His dad was his constant companion, tutor and fan. Part of his dad's way of teaching was to go with him to watch the Reds play at Crosley Field, a few blocks from their home. His father told him to watch second baseman Johnny Temple. Johnny was small in stature, but fast and aggressive. "Johnny has to fight for everything he gets," his dad told him.

Pete, too, had to make the most of his own size and special skills, for he was not always as husky as he is now. He had to become a scrappy player, able to take advantage of every break. His father saw to it that he became a switchhitter, so that he could bat right-handed against left-handers and left-handed against right-handed pitchers. That way, curve balls always break toward him, rather than away from him and out of reach.

The Roses watched a lot of baseball on television, too. One day in 1950 Pete and his dad were watching a game. The Reds were playing the St. Louis Cardinals, and Enos Slaughter was playing for the Cards. Enos was one of the original "Gas-House Gang." They regularly turned ordinary baseball games upside-down. They hit, clowned, made magical plays in the field, and, above all, ran the bases like demons.

As the Roses were watching, Enos was awarded a base on balls. But he did not "take a walk." Slaughter sprinted to first! Pete was astounded. His Dad was delighted. He said, "*There,* Pete! That's the way to play baseball! A little hustle can make up for a lot of mistakes."

Hustle is Pete's trademark. He is known everywhere as "Charley Hustle." Legend has it that this nickname was bestowed on him by two Yankees who saw him for the first time in spring training in 1963. They saw him running, throwing and working hard at every phase of his game. They could not believe their eyes.

They were watching a throwback to turn-of-the-century baseball. They did not think anyone played baseball that way any more!

Perhaps these observers had become too accustomed to their own sophisticated type of play. The Yankees, with their lineup of powerful hitters and consistent pitchers, didn't think they had to stir up the dust when they played. Anyway, Mickey Mantle and Whitey Ford stood behind the batting cage, watching Pete run and holler. Mantle asked, "What is *that*?" And Ford replied, "I don't know, but I got a name for it. Charley Hustle." The name stuck.

Pete still runs hard everywhere he goes on the playing field. He doesn't stop hurrying when he approaches a base, and often slides in head first, creating enough dust to cover a Little League infield. Pete says a head-first slide is the fastest way to get to a base. He doesn't have to change his momentum in order to tuck his legs for a feet-first slide. And he avoids injury to his legs and ankles.

Those who know how well the name "Charley Hustle" fits him must have been startled when he admitted that he didn't always hustle. In 1966 he was told to play third base, after having three very good seasons at second. He had, in fact, been good enough to be recognized as the best second baseman in the league.

But he was stubborn about moving, and didn't accept the new assignment: "I didn't work hard at it. I didn't give it my best shot." He played third for three weeks, and hit only .170 while there. The manager moved him back to second base, which turned out to be a happy choice. Pete wound up the season hitting .313, scored 97 times, and hit safely 205 times.

In 1967, however, he did accept a move to right field when Tommy Helms came to the Reds to play second. Pete worked hard at his new position, and developed an unorthodox but very effective way of catching flyballs. He reaches out as the ball is coming down and seems to snatch it out of the air, as though it was passing by him on a fast-moving conveyor belt.

He soon became an outstanding outfielder. He won Gold Glove awards in 1969 and 1970 for being the best fielder in his position. He also has the best lifetime fielding average for outfielders who have played 1000 or more games, .9919.

Pete has not been playing third base very long. He was moved to that position in May, 1975, so that George Foster could play full time in the outfield. The change also strengthened the infield at the corners. As soon as he started playing third and Foster began hitting the long ball, the Reds came to life. They were virtually unstoppable for the rest of the season.

As a third baseman, Pete covers a lot of ground on balls hit to his left and is like a vacuum cleaner on balls hit down the third base line. On a bunt he comes in like a hungry bear, concentrates, scoops and throws. Pitchers do not contest his right to rule the third-base side of the infield. They duck.

Pete still gets as excited about playing as he did when his dad was cheering him on. In many ways, he is like the kid he once was.

A story told by Carleton Fisk, the Red Sox catcher, captures this side of Pete. It was in the sixth game of the 1975 World Series, a game that all by itself had enough heart-stopping plays and dramatic moments for a whole season. Even people who never watch baseball heard about it and tuned in.

For Pete, a game like that was what baseball was all about. He came to the plate in the tenth inning, wanting to get something going for the Reds. He clapped his hands free of dirt, and squeezed the pine tar on his bat. But then he looked around at the crowd, at the scoreboard, and grinned. He turned to Fisk: "Hey. This is *some* kind of game, isn't it?"

Fisk knew exactly what he meant, and knew that Pete was the right man to say it. Pete Rose is some kind of ballplayer.

superstars!
superstars!
superstars!

CREATIVE EDUCATION SPORTS SUPERSTARS

Football
Johnny Unitas
Bob Griese
Vince Lombardi
Joe Namath
O. J. Simpson
Fran Tarkenton
Roger Staubach
Alan Page
Larry Csonka
Don Shula
Franco Harris
Terry Bradshaw
Chuck Foreman

Baseball
Frank Robinson
Tom Seaver
Jackie Robinson
Johnny Bench
Hank Aaron
Roberto Clemente
Mickey Mantle
Rod Carew
Fred Lynn
Pete Rose

Basketball
Walt Frazier
Kareem Abdul Jabbar
Wilt Chamberlain
Jerry West
Bill Russell
Bill Walton
Bob McAdoo
Julius Erving
John Havlicek
Rick Barry
George McGinnis

Golf
Lee Trevino
Jack Nicklaus
Arnold Palmer
Johnny Miller
Kathy Whitworth
Laura Baugh

Miscellaneous
Mark Spitz
Muhammad Ali
Secretariat
Olga Korbut
Evel Knievel
Jean Claude Killy
Janet Lynn
Peggy Fleming
Pelé
Rosi Mittermaier
Sheila Young
Dorothy Hamill
Nadia Comaneci

Tennis
Jimmy Connors
Chris Evert
Pancho Gonzales
Evonne Goolagong
Arthur Ashe
Billie Jean King
Stan Smith

Hockey
Phil and Tony Esposito
Gordie Howe
Bobby Hull
Bobby Orr

Racing
Peter Revson
Jackie Stewart
A. J. Foyt
Richard Petty